# Vim Essen

Eric Frick

Published by Eric Frick 2023

Last Update December 2023

# Copyright

# Foreword

Hello and welcome to the book! I have been programming and have worked on Linux (and Unix) systems for almost 40 years. Throughout my years as a developer, I have used the Vim editor off and on for a very long time. I always felt like I had to hunt around to find out more details on how to get the most out of using the Vim editor. That is why I put this book together.

I wanted to write a simple, straightforward book that explains how to get the most from using the Vim editor. I did not want to write a giant book that you would use as a doorstop that you could never get through. Rather, I wanted to build a short, concise book that would get you going with Vim right away and you could also use as a reference if you ever needed to look up a command.

By purchasing this book, you will also get access to an online video version of this course on my website. In this course, I will show the various features of Vim and have also included online labs that you can practice with without having to install any software. I firmly believe in learning by doing and my online lab environment does just that. I will include more details about the labs in a later chapter, but if you want to check it out, you can visit the lab at the following URL:

http://labs.destinlearning.com

Again, thank you for purchasing the book. I'm glad you are here! If you have any feedback for me or suggestions on how to improve the book/video course. You can contact me at: sales@destinglearning.com

# Contents

# Chapter 1 - Introduction to VIM

# Vim
# Essentials

GETTING STARTED WITH
THE VIM EDITOR

```
</li>
<li ui-sref-active="GDPR General Data Protection Regulation"
    ng-if="$ctrl.hasPermissionToEdit()">
    <a ui-sref="data.edit({id: $ctrl.project.id})" translate="data.EDITOR_TITLE"><
</li>
<li ng-if="!$ctrl.project.template"
    ui-sref-active="GDPR General Data Protection Regulation"
    has-permission-to="GDPR General Data Protection Regulation">
    <a ui-sref="data.dataProcessing({id: $ctrl.project.id})"
       translate="data.DATA_PROCESSING"></a>
</li>
</ul>
<a href="javascript:void(0)" ng-click="$ctrl.history.undo()"
   ng-disabled="!$ctrl.history.hasPrevious()"
   ng-if="$ctrl.hasPermissionToEdit()"
   title="{{'GDPR' | translate}}">
   <i class="material-icons toolbar-icon">undo</i>
</a>
<a href="javascript:void(0)" ng-click="$ctrl.history.redo()" ng-disabled="!$ctrl.hist
   ng-if="$ctrl.hasPermissionToEdit()"
   title="{{'GDPR' | translate}}">
   <i class="material-icons toolbar-icon">redo</i>
</a>
</div>
```

Eric Frick

1

# 1.1 Course Introduction

Vim, renowned for its comprehensive capabilities, stands as a text editor par excellence, having graced the computing world for over three decades. Its allure lies in an extensive array of advanced features such as macros, syntax highlighting, and the capacity to handle multiple files at once. Despite its many virtues, Vim's complexity presents a formidable challenge to new users, with a learning curve that can be quite steep.

"Vim Essentials" is crafted as a navigational tool through the intricate landscape of Vim, offering a detailed roadmap for both beginners and experts. Structured into six methodically arranged chapters, it systematically unpacks the intricacies of Vim:

1. **Introduction to Vim**: This opening chapter sets the stage, tracing Vim's historical roots and elucidating its wide-ranging capabilities.
2. **Basic Editing**: Here, the foundational elements of Vim are explored, guiding readers through navigation, text editing, and the quintessential copy/paste commands.
3. **Advanced Editing**: Venturing deeper, this section delves into the more sophisticated aspects of Vim, such as macros, complex search-replace functions, and managing multiple files concurrently.
4. **Customizing Vim**: This segment is dedicated to personalizing Vim, tailoring the interface and configurations to the user's individual tastes and preferences.

5. **Macros in Vim**: Demonstrating the efficiency of macros, this chapter reveals how to automate repetitive tasks, thereby boosting productivity within Vim.
6. **Using Vim for Coding and Troubleshooting Vim**: The final chapter tackles the specifics of employing Vim for coding tasks, emphasizing syntax highlighting and code folding, alongside pragmatic solutions for common troubleshooting scenarios within Vim.

Central to "Vim Essentials" is its hands-on approach, incorporating lab exercises to provide practical experience and reinforce learning. By engaging with these exercises, readers can apply the concepts in real-time, solidifying their understanding through practice.

This book stands as a thorough guide to mastering the potent text editor that is Vim. By its end, readers will be well-versed in the myriad features of Vim and equipped to utilize them to their full extent, ensuring a highly efficient and productive editing workflow.

# 1.2 Introduction to Vim

Vim, short for Vi IMproved, is an advanced text editor that is an extension of the original Vi editor. It is designed for efficient text editing and is widely used in the Unix and Linux communities, although it is available on almost all operating systems. Vim is not just another text editor; it is known for its power, flexibility, and efficiency, especially in the hands of an experienced user.

**History and Evolution**

Vim was first released in 1991 by Bram Moolenaar and has since evolved with contributions from a vibrant community. It started as a clone of the Vi editor but added improvements and new features over time. Today, it remains one of the most popular text editors among developers, system administrators, and writers who appreciate its modal nature and extendibility.

**Core Features**

- **Modality**: Vim operates in various modes, primarily Normal, Insert, and Visual, each with a specific purpose, allowing for a unique workflow that reduces unnecessary keystrokes.

- **Customization**: Users can customize Vim extensively through its vimrc configuration file, tailoring the editor to personal preferences and workflows.

- **Portability**: Vim is available on a wide range of platforms, making it a reliable tool for users who work across different systems.

- **Extensibility**: Vim supports plugins and scripts, enabling the addition of new features or the enhancement of existing ones.

- **Automation**: Vim's macros and automation capabilities allow users to record and play sequences of commands to perform complex editing tasks quickly.

- **Community and Support**: A large and active community means users have access to a wealth of plugins, scripts, tutorials, and support resources.

**Why Learn Vim?**

Despite its steep learning curve, learning Vim can be rewarding:

- **Efficiency**: Once mastered, Vim's command combinations can make text editing significantly faster.

- **Availability**: Vim is standard on macOS and most Unix systems, and available for download on Windows.

- **Productivity**: Vim's powerful features can be combined to handle complex editing tasks that go beyond the capabilities of ordinary text editors.

- **Control**: Vim provides a high level of control over text editing, which is appealing to those who like to have fine-grained control over their environment.

**Hands-On Lab Exercises**

"Vim Essentials" includes hands-on lab exercises at the end of each chapter, allowing readers to practice Vim commands and concepts in a controlled environment. These exercises are designed to reinforce learning and build muscle memory for the commands taught.

**Summary**

This chapter serves as a gateway to understanding Vim. It gives an overview of Vim's origins, core features, and the benefits of integrating it into your daily workflow. The upcoming chapters and lab exercises will equip you with the knowledge and practice needed to navigate Vim confidently and make the most of its rich feature set. Whether you're new to text editing or an experienced coder looking for an edge, Vim has the potential to significantly enhance your editing capabilities.

# 1.3 Destin Learning Lab Environment

 Welcome to Destin Learning Labs!

Welcome to Destin Learning Labs, where you have the opportunity to learn technology hands-on. We firmly believe in learning by doing. On this website we have constructed a series of hands-on labs for learning technologies like Linux, software development, cloud computing and more.

These labs compliment our online video courses. You can see our course catalog at:

https://courses.destinlearning.com

In this book, all the labs are available at the Destin Learning website as part of the online course. These labs are integrated directly into the course, and you do not need to install any software. Installing necessary software tools for programming is challenging for many students. This leads to wasted time and reduced focus on learning.

This lab is run on containers that don't save your files permanently, so remember to copy and paste your code to your home computer if you want to save it. In the future, I plan to add support for more advanced code editing using this lab.

The lab for this course is based on an embedded Linux terminal; you can issue any command that will run on a Linux environment if you are familiar with this. Don't worry if you have not used Linux before the lab has step-by step instructions on what to do.

## Linux Lab

In this environment, you will edit, compile, and run programs using the Linux command line. You will use the Vim editor to edit data files and source code. The format of the lab displays the instructions on the left-hand side and the editor on the terminal on the right-hand side.

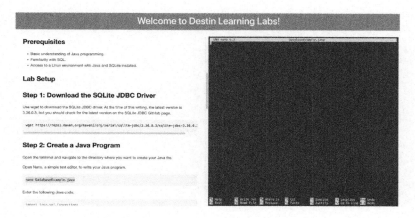

I have recently standardized on using the Linux environment exclusively for all my courses. Since Linux is open source, it is very affordable for me to host my labs. It is also the dominant technology used today in commercial computing and cloud computing environments.

You are certainly welcome to install and run Vim on your own home computer and run these labs. I've realized that it is more valuable for me to support a standard lab environment accessible to everyone, rather than troubleshooting students' personal devices. The lab also gives me a single place to test and troubleshoot code problems.

If you run into any problems with any of the labs, please contact me at:

sales@destinlearning.com

# 1.4 Installing Vim on Linux, Windows and MacOS

Vim is a versatile text editor that's available on a variety of platforms. Installation is straightforward, but the process varies slightly depending on your operating system. This chapter will guide you through the installation of Vim on Linux, Windows, and MacOS.

### Installing Vim on Linux

Vim is usually pre-installed on most Linux distributions. If not, it can easily be installed via the package manager.

**Debian-based systems (like Ubuntu)**:
```
sudo apt-get update
sudo apt-get install vim
```

**Red Hat-based systems (like Fedora and CentOS)**:
```
sudo dnf install vim
```

**Arch Linux**:
```
sudo pacman -S vim
```

**Installing Vim on Windows**

For Windows users, Vim needs to be downloaded
and installed manually.

- **Download Vim for Windows**: Go to the
  official Vim website and download the
  executable installer.
- **Run the Installer**: Execute the downloaded
  file and follow the on-screen instructions to
  install Vim.

Additionally, Windows users can also install Vim
through package managers like Chocolatey:

```
choco install vim
```

## Installing Vim on MacOS

Vim comes pre-installed on MacOS, but the pre-installed version might be outdated. To install the latest version:

- **Using Homebrew**:
  - `brew install vim`

- **MacPorts**:
  - `sudo port install vim`

## Post-Installation Steps

After installing Vim, it's a good practice to verify the installation.

- **Check Vim Version**: Type `vim --version` in the terminal (Linux/MacOS) or command prompt (Windows) to check the installed version.

- **Open Vim**: Simply type `vim` in the terminal or command prompt, and you should be greeted with the Vim welcome screen.

**Summary**

Installing Vim is the first step to leveraging its powerful features for text editing. Whether you are on Linux, Windows, or MacOS, getting Vim set up is a matter of a few commands or clicks. Once installed, you can start exploring Vim's capabilities, and with the help of this guide, you'll be navigating and editing files in Vim in no time. Remember to check for updates regularly to ensure you have the latest features and security fixes.

# 1.5 Launching and Exiting the Vim Editor

For those new to Vim, starting and exiting the editor can be less intuitive compared to GUI-based text editors. This chapter will guide you through the process of launching Vim and exiting it properly, ensuring that your work is saved and that you feel comfortable navigating this initial step in your Vim journey.

**Launching Vim**

To start editing with Vim, you can launch it from the command line:

- **On Linux and MacOS**: Open your terminal, and you can launch Vim in several ways:
    - Type `vim` to start Vim with a blank document.
    - Type `vim filename` to open an existing file or create a new one with the specified name.
- **On Windows**: Open the Command Prompt or PowerShell, and use the same commands as above.

**Exiting Vim**

Exiting Vim is done through command-line mode, which you enter by pressing `:` while in Normal Mode. Here are the primary commands:

- **Quit Without Saving Changes**: Type `:q!` and press `Enter` to exit Vim without saving any changes. The exclamation mark (!) forces Vim to quit, discarding any unsaved changes.
- **Save Changes and Quit**: Type `:wq` or `:x` and press `Enter`. The `w` stands for write (save), and `q` stands for quit. You can also save with `:w` and then quit with `:q`.
- **Save Changes**: If you want to save the changes but keep working, type `:w`, followed by the `Enter` key. You can also provide a new filename to save the current file with a different name using `:w newfilename`.

**Saving and Exiting in One Go**

You can combine saving and quitting into a single command:

- **Save and Quit**: Type `:wq` or `ZZ` (in Normal Mode without the colon) to save changes and exit.

## Exiting Vim When Multiple Files Are Open

If you have multiple files open (in buffers or tabs), you'll need to close each one or use a command to quit all:

- **Close All and Quit**: Type `:qa!` to quit all open files without saving changes, or `:wqa` to save all changes and then quit.

## Handling Unresponsive Vim

On rare occasions, Vim might become unresponsive:

- **Force Quit**: In the terminal, you can force Vim to close by typing `killall vim` on Linux/MacOS or closing the Command Prompt/PowerShell window on Windows.

## Summary

Launching and exiting Vim is straightforward once you're familiar with the commands. Remembering these basic commands will ensure that you can start and finish your editing sessions without losing data. As you become more comfortable with Vim, these commands will become second nature, and exiting Vim will be just as easy as any other text editor.

# 1.6 Lab - Launching and Exiting the Vim Editor

**Introduction**

One of the initial skills to master in Vim is starting and exiting the editor confidently. This lab is designed to provide hands-on practice with these fundamental operations. You will learn to open Vim, navigate through its modes, save your work, and exit the editor.

**Objectives**

- Learn how to launch Vim from the command line.
- Understand how to open files in Vim.
- Practice saving changes to your work.
- Master the commands for exiting Vim.

**Step-by-Step Exercises**

**Exercise 1: Launching Vim**

1. **Objective**: Open Vim to start a new text editing session.
2. **Task**: Open your terminal (or Command Prompt/PowerShell in Windows).
3. **Action**: Type `vim` and press `Enter`. This will open Vim with a new blank document.

## Exercise 2: Opening a File in Vim

1. **Objective**: Learn how to open an existing file or create a new one.

2. **Task**: With the terminal still open, type `vim example.txt` and press `Enter`.

3. **Action**: If the file exists, Vim will open it; if not, Vim will start a new buffer with the name `example.txt` ready for you to edit.

## Exercise 3: Saving Your Work

1. **Objective**: Save changes made to the file.

2. **Task**: Type `i` to switch to Insert Mode. Enter some text, then press `Esc` to return to Normal Mode.

3. **Action**: Type `:w` followed by `Enter` to save your changes.

### Exercise 4: Exiting Vim

1. **Objective**: Exit Vim after you have finished editing.

2. **Task**: From Normal Mode, type `:q` and press `Enter`.

3. **Action**: If you have unsaved changes, Vim will warn you. Save your changes using `:w` and repeat the exit command, or use `:q!` to exit without saving.

### Exercise 5: Saving and Exiting Simultaneously

1. **Objective**: Combine the save and exit operations into one command.

2. **Task**: Open Vim again with `vim example.txt`, insert some text, and return to Normal Mode.

3. **Action**: Type `:wq` and press `Enter` to save your changes and exit Vim in one step.

### Exercise 6: Force Quitting Vim

1. **Objective**: Force Vim to quit in cases where normal exit commands do not work.

2. **Task**: Open Vim with `vim example.txt`, make some changes but do not save.

3. **Action**: Type `:q!` and press `Enter` to force Vim to quit without saving the changes.

## Summary

Through these exercises, you should now be comfortable with opening Vim, editing files, saving your work, and exiting the editor. Remembering these simple yet crucial commands will provide a solid foundation as you continue to learn and explore the powerful features of Vim. With practice, these operations will become a natural part of your text editing workflow, allowing you to focus on more advanced Vim functionalities.

# Chapter 2 - Basic Concepts of Vim

# 2.1 Navigation in Vim

Navigating within a file is an important part of using the Vim editor effectively. Vim provides several ways to navigate through a file, including moving the cursor by character, word, or line, scrolling the view, and jumping to specific locations in the file. By becoming familiar with the navigation features in Vim, users can work more efficiently and productively with their files.

Here are some common navigation commands in Vim:

**Basic Movement**

- **h, j, k, l**: Basic navigation keys for moving left, down, up, and right.
- **0 and $**: Jump to the beginning or end of a line.

**Moving by Words and Sentences**

- **w, e, b**: Navigate through words.
- **( and )**: Move by sentences.

**Paragraphs and Sections**

- **{ and }**: Navigate by paragraphs.
- **and**: Jump between sections.

**Scrolling the View**

- **Ctrl-U and Ctrl-D**: Scroll half a page.
- **Ctrl-B and Ctrl-F**: Scroll a full page.

### Jumping to Specific Locations

- **G, gg, :[number]G**: Go to end, start, or a specific line in the file.

- **%**: Jump to matching brackets or parentheses.

### Search-Based Navigation

- **/ and ?**: Search within the file.

- **\*** and #\*\***: Find next or previous occurrences of a word.

### Marks and Jumps

- **m[letter] and `[letter]**: Set and jump to marks.

- **Ctrl-O and Ctrl-I**: Navigate through the jump list.

### Summary

Efficient navigation in Vim is essential for productivity. This chapter covers the fundamental navigation commands, including basic movement, word and sentence navigation, paragraph and section jumps, scrolling, specific location jumps, search-based navigation, and the use of marks and jumps. These tools transform the way users interact with text, making editing tasks quicker and more efficient. Practicing these commands is key to developing proficiency in Vim.

## 2.2 Basic Editing Commands in Vim

This section introduces the fundamental editing commands in Vim. Understanding these commands is vital for efficient text manipulation and forms the core of the Vim editing experience.

**Inserting Text**

- **i**: Enter insert mode before the cursor.
- **I**: Insert at the beginning of the line.
- **a**: Append after the cursor.
- **A**: Append at the end of the line.
- **o**: Open a new line below the current line.
- **O**: Open a new line above the current line.

**Deleting Text**

- **x**: Delete the character under the cursor.
- **dw**: Delete a word.
- **dd**: Delete the entire line.
- **d$**: Delete to the end of the line.
- **D**: Same as d$, delete to the end of the line.

**Copying and Pasting Text**

- **yy** or **Y**: Copy (yank) the current line.
- **yw**: Yank a word.
- **p**: Paste after the cursor.
- **P**: Paste before the cursor.

**Undo and Redo**

- **u**: Undo the last operation.
- **Ctrl-R**: Redo the last undone operation.

**Other Editing Commands**

- **r**: Replace a single character.
- **cw**: Change (replace) a word.
- **cc** or **S**: Change (replace) the entire line.
- **~**: Toggle case of a character.
- **J**: Join the current line with the next line.
- **>>** and **<<**: Indent and unindent a line.

**Summary**

This chapter covers the basic editing commands in Vim, including inserting text, deleting text, copying and pasting, and undoing and redoing changes. These commands are the building blocks for text editing in Vim. Mastery of these commands allows for efficient and quick text manipulation, greatly enhancing the editing process. Remember, practice is key to becoming proficient in using these commands seamlessly during your editing workflow.

# 2.3: Lab - Basic Editing Commands in Vim

**Introduction**

This lab session is aimed at providing a hands-on experience with Vim's basic editing commands, using a practical exercise to enhance your understanding and skill.

**Step 1: Setting up a Sample Data File by Copy and Paste**

- **Create a New File**: Open Vim and create a new file by typing `:e sample.txt`.

- **Copy Sample Data**: Use the following sample text or find another suitable excerpt:
  - The quick brown fox jumps over the lazy dog.
  - Lorem ipsum dolor sit amet, consectetur adipiscing elit.
  - Vim is a highly efficient text editor.

- **Paste into Vim**: Enter insert mode (`i`), paste the copied text, and save the file with `:w`.

**Step 2: Inserting Text**

- Experiment with different insert commands (`i`, `I`, `a`, `A`, `o`, `O`) to add text like "This is a new sentence." in various places.

**Step 3: Deleting Text**

- Practice using `x` to delete characters, `dw` to delete words, `dd` to delete lines, and `d$` or `D` to delete to the end of a line.

### Step 4: Copying and Pasting Text

- Copy lines with yy or Y and words with yw. Then, use p and P to paste the copied content in different locations.

### Step 5: Undo and Redo

- Utilize u to undo your changes and Ctrl-R to redo the last undone operation.

### Step 6: Other Editing Commands

- Replace characters with r, change words or entire lines with cw, cc, or S. Toggle the case of characters using ~ and join lines with J. Practice indenting (>>) and unindenting (<<) lines.

### Summary

This lab provided a structured approach to practicing Vim's basic editing commands. By following these steps and working with the sample text, you've gained practical experience in inserting, deleting, copying, pasting, and other editing operations. Regular practice of these commands will enhance your efficiency and fluency in using Vim for text editing.

## 2.4 Modes in the Vim Editor

Vim, unlike most text editors, operates in several different modes. Each mode is optimized for a set of tasks, allowing for efficient text manipulation and command execution. Understanding these modes is crucial for any Vim user, as it enables you to harness the full power of this versatile editor. This chapter will delve into the primary modes of Vim, explaining their purposes and how to navigate between them.

### Normal Mode

- **Overview**: Normal Mode is Vim's starting point; it's where you can run commands to manipulate text and navigate through the file.

- **Usage**: To perform actions like moving the cursor, deleting text, and copying and pasting text.

- **Commands**: Navigation commands (h, j, k, l), editing commands (dd for deleting a line, yy for copying a line), and more complex combinations for multi-step operations.

- **Entering Normal Mode**: Simply press Esc from any other mode.

### Insert Mode

- **Overview**: Insert Mode turns Vim into a standard text editor where you can type and edit text naturally.

- **Usage**: To insert text at the cursor's location.

- **Features**: You can insert new text, correct mistakes, or add content anywhere in the document.

29

- **Entering Insert Mode**: Press i from Normal Mode. Other variations like I (insert at the beginning of the line), a (append after the cursor), and A (append at the end of the line) are also used.

### Visual Mode

- **Overview**: Visual Mode allows for text selection using Vim's navigation commands.

- **Usage**: To perform operations on a block of text, like indenting, copying, or deleting selected areas.

- **Types**: There are three types of Visual Mode:
  - Visual (v) for character selection.
  - Visual Line (V) for selecting whole lines.
  - Visual Block (Ctrl-V) for selecting blocks of text.

- **Entering Visual Mode**: Press v, V, or Ctrl-V from Normal Mode.

**Command-Line Mode**

- **Overview**: Command-Line Mode is where you can enter longer, more complex commands.
- **Usage**: To perform file and environment operations, such as saving files (`:w`), opening files (`:e`), setting options (`:set`), or running macros.
- **Features**: Command history is available, allowing you to scroll through and repeat previously executed commands.
- **Entering Command-Line Mode**: Press `:` from Normal Mode.

**Summary**

Understanding and utilizing the various modes in Vim is essential for efficient text editing. Normal Mode is the default and is optimized for navigating and manipulating text. Insert Mode allows for traditional text entry. Visual Mode provides a powerful way to select and operate on blocks of text. Command-Line Mode is for executing more complex file and editor commands. Mastering these modes and learning to switch between them seamlessly is a key step in becoming proficient with Vim. Each mode has its unique set of functions and commands, which together, provide a comprehensive editing environment.

# 2.5 Lab - How to Use Modes in the Vim Editor

**Introduction**

Vim's efficiency as a text editor stems from its modal design, which provides different environments tailored for specific tasks. This lab is designed to help you understand and utilize Vim's modes effectively, enhancing your editing workflow.

**Objectives**

- To gain a comprehensive understanding of Vim's different modes.

- To learn how to switch between Normal, Insert, Visual, and Command-Line Modes.

- To perform typical text-editing operations within each mode.

**Step 1: Explore Normal Mode**

- **Objective**: Become comfortable with navigation and basic editing in Normal Mode.

- **Task**: Open Vim, ensure you're in Normal Mode by pressing Esc, and practice navigating with h, j, k, l. Try deleting characters with x and lines with dd.

## Step 2: Enter Insert Mode

- **Objective**: Learn how to insert and edit text in Insert Mode.

- **Task**: Press i from Normal Mode to enter Insert Mode. Insert the following text:
  - Vim is an adventure. Each mode is a path to new capabilities.
  - Mastery of modes is mastery of text editing itself.

  After typing, press Esc to return to Normal Mode.

- **Variations**: Use I to insert text at the start of a line, a to append after the cursor, A to append at the end of the line, o to open a new line below, and 0 to open a new line above the current line.

## Step 3: Use Visual Mode

- **Objective**: Practice selecting and manipulating text using Visual Mode.

- **Task**: Enter Visual Mode by pressing v in Normal Mode, select some text, and perform an operation like deleting (d) or copying (y). Exit Visual Mode with Esc.

- **Types of Selection**: Also, use V for selecting whole lines and Ctrl-V for block selection. Try changing the selected text with operations like indenting (>) or applying a command (:).

**Step 4: Experiment with Command-Line Mode**

- **Objective**: Execute commands for file management and text processing.

- **Task**: Press `:` from Normal Mode to enter Command-Line Mode. Write changes with `:w`, quit with `:q`, search with `:/pattern`, and change settings with `:set option`. Try global replacement with `:%s/old/new/g`.

**Summary**

This lab has provided you with practical experience in the primary modes of Vim. You've learned that Normal Mode is for navigation and command execution, Insert Mode for text entry, Visual Mode for text selection, and Command-Line Mode for executing extended commands. By practicing with the sample text and commands provided, you're on your way to becoming proficient in Vim, ready to harness its full potential for efficient text editing.

## 2.6 How to Search for Text

Searching for text is a fundamental aspect of text editing, and Vim provides powerful tools for this purpose. Vim's search functionality is robust, offering precise navigation to specific pieces of text within a file. This section will explore the various search options in Vim, detailing how to use them to navigate efficiently and edit effectively.

**Forward Search**

- **Usage**: To search for text after the cursor's position.

- **Command**: /pattern – After typing /, enter the text pattern you wish to find and press Enter.

- **Navigating Results**: Use n to move to the next occurrence and N to move to the previous occurrence.

**Backward Search**

- **Usage**: To search for text before the cursor's position.

- **Command**: ?pattern – Similar to forward search, but searches backward.

- **Navigating Results**: n moves to the previous occurrence, while N moves to the next occurrence, reversing the direction compared to forward search.

## Case Sensitivity

- **Ignoring Case**: `:set ignorecase` – Makes searches case-insensitive.

- **Smart Case**: `:set smartcase` – Searches are case-insensitive unless the pattern contains uppercase characters.

- **Overriding Case Sensitivity**: Adding `\c` (ignore case) or `\C` (match case) to a search pattern overrides the default behavior.

## Using Regular Expressions

- **Power of Regex**: Vim supports regular expressions, allowing complex pattern matching.

- **Special Characters**: Use special characters like `.` (any character), `*` (zero or more of the preceding character), `[]` (any one of the characters inside the brackets), etc.

### Whole Word Search

- **Command**: `/\` – Use \ before and after the pattern to search for the whole word.

- **Example**: `/\` – Finds "vim" as a separate word, not as part of another word like "vimrc".

### Highlighting Search Results

- **Enabling**: `:set hlsearch` – Highlights all occurrences of the search pattern.

- **Disabling**: `:nohlsearch` or `:set nohlsearch` – Turns off the highlighting until the next search.

### Incremental Search

- **Enabling**: `:set incsearch` – Shows matches for a pattern as you type it.

- **Usage**: Particularly useful for refining searches before completing the pattern.

### Jump to Next/Previous Match

- **Commands**: `*` and `#` – Search for the word under the cursor and navigate to the next (`*`) or previous (`#`) occurrence.

## Summary

Vim's search functionality is an indispensable tool for navigating and editing text files. It goes beyond simple text matching to include powerful options like case sensitivity controls, regular expression capabilities, whole word searching, and search result highlighting. Incremental search enhances the user experience by providing immediate feedback as you type your search query. By understanding and using these search options, you can significantly improve your efficiency in locating and manipulating text within Vim. The ability to quickly find and replace text can transform your editing workflow, making Vim a more powerful ally in your text editing endeavors.

# 2.7 Lab - Searching for Text in the Vim Editor

## Introduction

The ability to swiftly find and navigate to text within Vim is one of the keys to efficient text editing. This lab focuses on the various search functionalities Vim offers and will guide you through using them effectively. You'll learn not just to find text but also to utilize Vim's powerful pattern matching and search result management features.

## Objectives

- To set up a sample data file for search operations.
- To learn the basic forward and backward search commands.
- To understand and use case sensitivity and regular expressions in searches.
- To practice highlighting and navigating search results.
-

## Step 1: Set Up a Sample Data File

- **Objective**: Prepare a text file with diverse content to practice searching.
- **Task**: Open Vim and create a new file by typing `:e search_sample.txt`. Enter Insert Mode (`i`) and paste the following sample data:

Vim is a highly configurable text
editor built to enable efficient
text editing.
It is an improved version of the
vi editor distributed with most
UNIX systems.
Vim is rock—stable and is
continuously being developed to
become even better.
Among its features are syntax
highlighting, a comprehensive help
system, native scripting
(Vimscript), and support for
numerous programming languages and
file formats.
The bird is powered by its own
motivation to fly, much like Vim's
users who are driven by their
passion for text editing.

Save the file with `:w` and return to Normal
Mode by pressing `Esc`.

### Step 2: Perform a Forward Search

- **Objective**: Execute a forward search to find text after the cursor.

- **Task**: Type `/Vim` and press `Enter`. Use `n` to find the next occurrence and `N` to find the previous one.

### Step 3: Perform a Backward Search

- **Objective**: Learn to search for text in the reverse direction.

- **Task**: Type `?editor` and press `Enter`. Use `n` to navigate backward and `N` to navigate forward through the occurrences.

### Step 4: Explore Case Sensitivity in Search

- **Objective**: Understand how case sensitivity affects search results.

- **Task**: First, ensure case sensitivity is on with `:set noignorecase`. Search for `vim` with `/vim` and observe the results. Then, use `:set ignorecase` and search again with `/vim`.

### Step 5: Utilize Regular Expressions

- **Objective**: Use regular expressions for complex pattern matching.

- **Task**: Type `/\v\` to search for the word "is" as a whole word. Then, try searching for any five-letter word with `/\<\w\w\w\w\w\>`.

### Step 6: Highlight Search Results

- **Objective**: Learn to manage the visibility of search results.

- **Task**: Enable highlighting with `:set hlsearch` and perform a search. Turn off highlighting with `:nohlsearch`.

### Step 7: Incremental Search

- **Objective**: Experience real-time feedback while typing search patterns.

- **Task**: Activate incremental search with `:set incsearch`. Start typing a search pattern and observe how Vim highlights matches as you type.

**Summary**

In this lab, you have learned how to search for text in Vim using various techniques. You set up a sample data file and practiced forward and backward searches, managed case sensitivity, experimented with regular expressions, and navigated through highlighted results. Incremental search provided a dynamic way to see potential matches as you compose your search pattern. These search capabilities, when mastered, greatly enhance your editing workflow in Vim, allowing you to locate and modify text with precision and ease.

# Chapter 3 - Advanced Editing in Vim

# 3.1 Advanced Editing Commands

While Vim is renowned for its efficiency with basic text manipulation, it also boasts a rich set of advanced editing commands. These commands allow for complex operations and text transformations that can be executed with just a few keystrokes. This section dives into some of these advanced commands, offering detailed examples to showcase their power and utility.

### Global Replacement

* **Command**: `:%s/old/new/g`
* **Example**: To replace all instances of "foo" with "bar" throughout the entire file, you would use `:%s/foo/bar/g`.

### Joining Lines

* **Command**: `J`
* **Example**: To join the current line with the next line, simply press `J` while in Normal Mode. If you want to join the next three lines, you could press `3J`.

### Changing Case

* **Command**: `g~`, `gu`, `gU`
* **Example**: To change the case of the current word to uppercase, use `gUiw`. To change the entire line to lowercase, use `gu$`.

## Working with Tabs and Indents

- **Command**: >, <
- **Example**: To indent the current line, use >>. To unindent, use <<. To indent four lines below the cursor, use 4>>.

## Macros

- **Command**: q
- **Example**: To record a macro that changes the next word to uppercase, press qq, then gUw, and then q to stop recording. Execute it with @q.

## Marks

- **Command**: m, '
- **Example**: To mark the current position as mark 'a', press ma. To return to this position, press 'a.

## Conditional Search and Replace

- **Command**: :g/pattern/s/old/new/g
- **Example**: To replace "vim" with "VIM" on lines containing "editor", use :g/editor/s/vim/VIM/g.

## Advanced Movement

- **Command**: {, }
- **Example**: To move to the beginning of the paragraph, use {. To move to the end, use }.

### Using Buffers

- **Command**: `:b`, `:ls`
- **Example**: To list all open files (buffers), use `:ls`. To switch to buffer number 2, use `:b 2`.

### Window Management

- **Command**: `:split`, `:vsplit`
- **Example**: To split the window horizontally, use `:split`. To split it vertically, use `:vsplit`.

### Summary

Vim's advanced editing commands offer an extension to the basic commands, enabling you to perform more complex text manipulations with ease. Whether you're globally replacing text, managing indents, recording macros for repetitive tasks, or navigating through your text with precision, Vim has a command to streamline the process. These advanced capabilities not only speed up the editing process but also bring a level of finesse to text manipulation. The examples provided serve as a starting point for exploring the depth of Vim's functionality. With practice, these advanced commands will become a vital part of your Vim toolkit, empowering you to edit text with unparalleled efficiency.

# 3.2 Lab – Mastering Advanced Editing Features in the Vim Editor

## Introduction

Vim is not just a text editor; it's a powerful engine for text transformation, capable of executing complex tasks with simple commands. This lab is designed to teach you how to leverage Vim's advanced editing features through practical exercises. By the end of this lab, you'll be equipped to handle sophisticated text manipulations with confidence and agility.

## Objectives

- Create a sample file to practice advanced editing techniques.
- Learn to perform global text replacements.
- Practice joining lines and changing text case.
- Use macros to automate repetitive tasks.
- Set and jump to marks for quick navigation.
- Execute conditional search and replace.
- Manipulate text with advanced movement commands.
- Manage multiple files with buffers and windows.

### Step 1: Create a Sample Data File

- **Objective**: Establish a foundation for practicing advanced editing commands.

- **Task**: Open Vim and create a new file by typing `:e advanced_editing.txt`. Populate it with the following text:

```
Vim is not just a text editor, it's an experience.
It offers more than just text editing; it offers a
journey.
Vim's capabilities are only limited by one's
knowledge.
The text editing experience in Vim is unmatched.
To learn Vim is to learn a new way of thinking.
```

Save the file with `:w` and ensure you're in Normal Mode by pressing `Esc`.

### Step 2: Global Replacement

- **Objective**: Understand how to replace text throughout the file.

- **Task**: Use `:%s/text/editor/g` to replace all instances of "text" with "editor".

### Step 3: Joining Lines

- **Objective**: Learn to combine lines for better text flow.

- **Task**: Join the second and third lines by placing the cursor on the second line and pressing J.

### Step 4: Changing Case

- **Objective**: Master the skill of changing the case of text.

- **Task**: Change the fourth line to uppercase using gUU and then revert to lowercase with guu.

### Step 5: Recording and Using Macros

- **Objective**: Automate repetitive tasks with macros.

- **Task**: Record a macro to append "Vim" at the end of each line. Press qa, move to the end of a line with $, enter Insert Mode with a, type " Vim", exit Insert Mode with Esc, and then stop recording with q. Apply the macro to the next line with @a.

### Step 6: Marks for Quick Navigation

- **Objective**: Navigate efficiently within the document using marks.

- **Task**: Mark the current position in the file with ma, move elsewhere, and then return to the marked position with 'a.

### Step 7: Conditional Search and Replace

- **Objective**: Execute search and replace operations based on conditions.
- **Task**: Replace "Vim" with "VIM" only on lines that contain "journey" using `:g/journey/s/Vim/VIM/g`.

### Step 8: Advanced Movement Commands

- **Objective**: Navigate through text using paragraph and section movements.
- **Task**: Move between paragraphs with { and }.

### Step 9: Using Buffers and Window Management

- **Objective**: Manage multiple files and views efficiently.
- **Task**: Open a new file with `:e newfile.txt`, switch between it and the previous file using `:b#`, and split windows with `:split` and `:vsplit`.

## Summary

In this lab, you've taken a significant leap towards mastering Vim by learning and practicing its advanced features. These commands are not mere text manipulations; they are the keystrokes of efficiency that can transform your text editing from routine to remarkable. The steps provided serve as a practical guide to understanding and applying each advanced feature, from global replacements to window management. As you incorporate these advanced commands into your daily use of Vim, you'll find that your editing becomes faster, your workflow smoother, and your control over text more precise. The key to Vim mastery lies in practice, and through these exercises, you are well on your way to becoming an adept Vim user.

# 3.3 Copying, Cutting, and Pasting Text

The ability to copy, cut, and paste text is a fundamental feature of any text editor. In Vim, these actions are more commonly referred to as yanking, deleting, and putting. This part of the guide will explain how to perform these actions and provide step-by-step examples to help you practice these essential skills in Vim.

### Copying (Yanking) Text

- **Yank a Line**: To copy a line, place the cursor on the line you wish to copy and press yy.

- **Yank Multiple Lines**: To copy multiple lines, place the cursor on the first line, type y followed by the motion. For example, y2j will yank the line you're on and the next two lines.

### Cutting (Deleting) Text

- **Delete a Line**: To cut a line, use dd. This deletes the line and stores it in Vim's buffer.

- **Delete a Word**: To cut a word, place the cursor at the beginning of the word and press dw.

### Pasting (Putting) Text

- **Paste After Cursor**: To paste text after the cursor, press p. This puts the yanked or deleted text after the current line or cursor position.

- **Paste Before Cursor**: To paste text before the cursor, press P.

### Step-by-Step Examples

### Example 1: Copy and Paste a Single Line

1. Move the cursor to the line you want to copy.
2. Press yy to yank the line.
3. Move the cursor to the location where you want to paste the copied line.
4. Press p to paste the line below the cursor or P to paste it above.

### Example 2: Cut and Paste a Block of Text

1. Enter Visual Mode by pressing v.
2. Use the arrow keys to select a block of text.
3. Press d to delete (cut) the selected text.
4. Move the cursor to the target paste location.
5. Press p to paste the text below the cursor or P to paste it above.

### Example 3: Copying and Pasting Multiple Lines

1. Place the cursor on the first line you want to copy.

2. Press 3yy to yank the current line plus the next two lines (total 3).

3. Move the cursor to where you want to paste these lines.

4. Press p to paste the lines below the cursor or P to paste them above.

### Summary

Copying, cutting, and pasting text in Vim can seem daunting at first due to its modal nature. However, once you learn the key commands (yy for yanking, dd for deleting, p and P for putting), it becomes second nature. Remembering that Vim uses a register to store the yanked or deleted text helps understand how the pasting process works. Vim's powerful visual mode further enhances these actions, allowing for precise text manipulation over large blocks with simple keystrokes. With practice, these commands will become an integral part of your Vim workflow, significantly speeding up text editing tasks.

# 3.4 Lab - Copying and Pasting Text Using the Vim Editor

## Introduction

In Vim, copying and pasting is an art form that, once mastered, can significantly expedite your workflow. This lab is designed to help you understand and practice the mechanics of copying (yanking), cutting (deleting), and pasting (putting) text within Vim. By the end of this lab, you will be adept at manipulating text in your files with ease.

## Objectives

- Set up a sample file with diverse content for editing exercises.
- Learn and practice the commands for copying and pasting text within Vim.
- Understand how to select text for copying and cutting using visual mode.

### Step 1: Set Up a Sample Data File

- **Objective**: Prepare a text file to practice copying and pasting operations.

- **Task**: Open Vim, create a new file (`:e sample_editing.txt`), and enter the following text in Insert Mode (`i`):

- 

```
Lorem ipsum dolor sit amet, consectetur adipiscing
elit.
Sed do eiusmod tempor incididunt ut labore et dolore
magna aliqua.
Ut enim ad minim veniam, quis nostrud exercitation
ullamco laboris nisi ut aliquip ex ea commodo
consequat.
Duis aute irure dolor in reprehenderit in voluptate
velit esse cillum dolore eu fugiat nulla pariatur.
Excepteur sint occaecat cupidatat non proident, sunt
in culpa qui officia deserunt mollit anim id est
laborum.
```

  Save the file with `:w` and return to Normal Mode (`Esc`).

### Step 2: Copy and Paste a Single Line

- **Objective**: Copy a line of text and paste it elsewhere in the file.

- **Task**: Navigate to the second line. Press yy to yank it. Move to the end of the file and press p to paste it below the current line.

- **Example**: Copying the "Sed do eiusmod..." line and pasting it after the last line.

### Step 3: Cut and Paste a Section of Text

- **Objective**: Cut (delete) a block of text and paste it in a new location.

- **Task**: Enter Visual Mode (v), select the third line by pressing j twice. Press d to cut the text. Navigate to the top of the file and press P to paste it before the first line.

- **Example**: Cutting the "Ut enim ad minim..." section and pasting it at the beginning.**Step 4: Copy and Paste Multiple Lines**

- **Objective**: Copy multiple lines of text and paste them within the file.

- **Task**: Position the cursor on the first line of the text. Press 3yy to yank the first three lines. Move to the last line of the file and press p to paste the copied lines below.

- **Example**: Yanking the first three lines of the "Lorem ipsum..." text and pasting them after the last line.

### Step 5: Copy and Paste Words

- **Objective**: Copy specific words or parts of a line and paste them.

- **Task**: Navigate to the first word of the third line. Enter Visual Mode (v), select the word "Ut" by moving the cursor over it, and press y to yank. Move the cursor to the end of the last line and press p to paste.

- **Example**: Copying the word "Ut" and pasting it at the end of the file.

## Summary

Through these exercises, you have learned the fundamental techniques of copying, cutting, and pasting text in Vim. These operations are not just about moving text around; they are about restructuring and refining your document efficiently. Yanking with yy, cutting with d in Visual Mode, and putting with p or P are powerful tools in your Vim skill set. As with any skill, practice is key—regular use of these commands will help embed them in your muscle memory, making text manipulation in Vim second nature.

# 3.5 Quiz - Advanced Editing Commands in Vim

**Question 1**

What is the command to replace all occurrences of the word "apple" with "orange" in the entire file?

A) `:s/apple/orange/g`
B) `:%s/apple/orange/`
C) `:%s/apple/orange/g`
D) `:g/apple/orange/`

**Question 2**

How do you join the current line and the next three lines into one in Vim?

A) `3J`
B) `J3`
C) `jjjJ`
D) `Jjjj`

**Question 3**

If you wanted to change the case of the entire line to uppercase, which command would you use?

A) `gUU`
B) `guu`
C) `gUgU`
D) `ggU`

## Question 4
To record a macro in Vim, which key do you press first?

A) m
B) r
C) q
D) a

## Question 5
Which command would you use to return to a previously marked position labeled 'k'?

A) mk
B) bk
C) 'k
D) goto k

## Question 6
What is the command to replace the word "Vim" with "VIM" only on lines that contain the word "editor"?

A) :%s/editor.*Vim/VIM/g
B) :g/editor/s/Vim/VIM/
C) :%g/editor/s/Vim/VIM/
D) :g/editor/s/Vim/VIM/g

## Question 7

How do you move to the beginning of the next
paragraph in Vim?

A) }
B) {{
C) [[
D) {


## Question 8

If you have multiple files open in Vim, how do you list
all the open buffers?

A) :ls
B) :buffers
C) :open
D) Both A and B

## Summary

This short quiz is designed to test your knowledge of
advanced Vim commands after completing the lab
section. Understanding these commands is crucial
for efficient navigation and editing in Vim. Regular
practice of these commands will reinforce your
memory, making your interaction with Vim more
effective and intuitive.

# Chapter 4 - Customizing Vim

# 4.1 Understanding the Vim Editor Configuration File

The Vim editor is highly customizable, largely thanks to its configuration file, often referred to as the `.vimrc` or `vimrc`. This file allows users to define settings, map keys, and automate tasks, effectively tailoring the editor to individual needs and preferences. Understanding how to craft and modify this file is crucial for any Vim user who wishes to optimize their editing environment.

**Location of the Vim Configuration File**

The location of the Vim configuration file can vary based on the operating system:

- **On Unix-like systems (Linux, MacOS)**: It's typically found in the home directory as `~/.vimrc`.

- **On Windows**: Vim looks for `_vimrc` in various locations, including the home directory (`$HOME\_vimrc`), the Vim installation directory (`$VIM\_vimrc`), or the user's profile directory.

## Structure of the `.vimrc` File

The `.vimrc` file is a script written in Vim's own scripting language. Here are the components you might find in a `.vimrc` file:

- **Settings**: You can set options that change Vim's behavior, such as `set number` to show line numbers or `set ignorecase` to make searches case-insensitive.

- **Key Mappings**: Custom key bindings can be defined to speed up common tasks, using commands like `nnoremap` for normal mode remaps.

- **Functions and Commands**: For more complex operations, you can define functions or command shortcuts.

- **Plugin Configuration**: If you use plugins, the `.vimrc` file is where you configure them to your liking.

- **Autocommands**: These are commands that Vim will run automatically in certain scenarios, like opening or saving a file.

## Editing the `.vimrc` File

To edit the `.vimrc` file, simply open it in Vim:

```
vim ~/.vimrc
```
As you make changes to your `.vimrc`, you can source it without restarting Vim by running `:source` `~/.vimrc` or using the shorthand `:so %` when the `.vimrc` file is currently open.

## Best Practices

When customizing your `.vimrc`, consider the following:

- **Commenting**: Add comments to your configurations for clarity. Comments start with a `"`.

- **Modularity**: Group related settings and mappings together.

- **Version Control**: Keep your `.vimrc` under version control to track changes and sync across machines.

## Troubleshooting

If you encounter issues after modifying your `.vimrc`:

- **Check for Typos**: Syntax errors can cause Vim to behave unexpectedly.

- **Isolate Changes**: Comment out recent changes to see if they are the cause of the issue.

- **Vim Documentation**: Use Vim's built-in help system (`:help option-list`) to understand settings.

**Summary**

The Vim configuration file is your central tool for customizing Vim to fit your workflow. By understanding its structure and learning to modify it, you can transform Vim from a simple text editor to a powerful integrated development environment tailored specifically to you. With careful management of the `.vimrc` file, you can create a Vim experience that enhances productivity and enjoyment in your daily tasks.

# 4.2 Lab - Making Settings in the Vim Configuration File

The `.vimrc` file is where Vim looks for startup commands. Customizing this file allows you to tailor Vim to your preferences and workflow. In this lab, you'll learn to edit `.vimrc` to change Vim's settings and observe how these changes affect your editing experience. You'll be guided through modifying basic settings and then testing those changes with a sample file.

**Objectives**

- Learn to open and edit the `.vimrc` file.
- Understand how to set and unset options in Vim.
- Apply changes and observe their effects on a Vim session.

**Exercise 1: Opening and Editing `.vimrc`**

1. **Objective**: Access your `.vimrc` file.

2. **Task**: Open the terminal and type `vim ~/.vimrc` to edit your configuration file.

3. **Action**: Once open, you're ready to start making changes.

**Exercise 2: Changing Basic Settings**

1. **Objective**: Set common options to enhance your text editing.

2. **Task**: Insert the following settings into your `.vimrc`:
   - Line numbering: `set number`
   - Syntax highlighting: `syntax on`
   - Tab spaces: `set tabstop=4 shiftwidth=4 expandtab`
   - Search case insensitivity: `set ignorecase`
   - Search result highlighting: `set hlsearch`

3. **Action**: Write the changes (`:w`) and quit Vim (`:q`).

**Exercise 3: Testing Changes with a Sample File**

1. **Objective**: Observe the effect of your new settings.

2. **Task**: Create a new file or open an existing one with `vim testfile`.

3. **Action**: Confirm that line numbers appear, tab spaces are set correctly, and your searches are case insensitive with highlighted results.

**Exercise 4: Disabling Settings Temporarily**

1. **Objective**: Learn to disable settings within a Vim session.

2. **Task**: Disable line numbering and highlighting for the current session.

3. **Action**: Enter the following commands in command mode:

   - Disable line numbering: `:set nonumber`

   - Disable search highlighting: `:nohlsearch`

**Exercise 5: Re-enabling Settings**

1. **Objective**: Re-enable settings without editing `.vimrc`.

2. **Task**: Turn the line numbering and search highlighting back on.

3. **Action**: Enter the following commands in command mode:

   - Enable line numbering: `:set number`

   - Enable search highlighting: `:set hlsearch`

**Summary**

By completing this lab, you've taken an important step in personalizing your Vim editor. The `.vimrc` file is the heart of Vim's customization, and mastering its settings opens up a world of efficiency and productivity. Remember, any changes made in `.vimrc` require you to either restart Vim or source the file with `:source ~/.vimrc`. The more you experiment with `.vimrc`, the more you'll be able to make Vim your own.

# 4.3 Configuring the Vim Interface

The Vim editor stands out for its versatility and high degree of customization. One aspect that can significantly impact your productivity and ease of use is the interface configuration. By customizing the Vim interface, you can create a comfortable and personalized editing environment that aligns with your preferences and workflow. This chapter delves into several ways you can tailor the Vim interface to suit your needs.

**Customizing Color Schemes**

One of the most noticeable aspects of Vim's interface is its color scheme. Vim comes with several built-in color schemes that you can switch between.

- **Changing Color Schemes**: Use `:colorscheme [scheme_name]` to switch color schemes. Replace `[scheme_name]` with the name of the color scheme, like `desert` or `elflord`.

- **Finding More Color Schemes**: You can find additional color schemes online and add them to your `.vim/colors` directory for even more options.

### Adjusting Text Display

Vim allows you to adjust how text is displayed, which can help reduce eye strain and make your work more enjoyable.

- **Line Numbering**: Use `set number` to display line numbers or `set relativenumber` for relative line numbers.

- **Syntax Highlighting**: Enable with `syntax on` for easier code comprehension.

- **Font and Text Size**: While Vim in the terminal uses the terminal's font settings, GUI versions like GVim allow changing the font directly with `set guifont=[font_name]:h[font_size]`.

### Managing Screen Real Estate

How Vim uses the screen space can affect your workflow, especially when working with multiple files or long codebases.

- **Split Windows**: Use `:split` and `:vsplit` to divide your workspace into separate windows.

- **Tabs**: Use `:tabnew [filename]` to open files in tabs for easier navigation between multiple files.

- **Status Line**: Customize the status line with `set statusline=[custom_format]` to display information like the filename, file type, and cursor position.

## Key Mappings and Shortcuts

Vim is keyboard-centric, and configuring key mappings can make you more efficient.

- **Custom Mappings**: Map new commands or shortcuts with `:nnoremap [key combination] [action]`.
- **Leader Key**: The Leader key is a special placeholder that can be combined with other keys for custom shortcuts. Set it with `let mapleader="[key]"`.

## Enhancing with Plugins

Plugins can add new elements to the Vim interface or change existing ones.

- **File Browsers**: Plugins like NERDTree add a file browser side panel.
- **Status Bars**: Airline or Lightline plugins provide enhanced status bars with additional information and aesthetics.

## Saving Interface Settings

Remember to add your interface configuration settings to your `.vimrc` file to ensure they persist across sessions.

**Summary**

Configuring the Vim interface is an essential part of setting up your development environment. By customizing aspects like color schemes, text display options, screen layout, and key mappings, you can create a workspace that feels intuitive and responsive. The ability to tailor every part of the Vim interface is one of the editor's greatest strengths, and taking the time to configure it to your liking can lead to a more pleasant and productive coding experience.

# 4.4 Changing Colors, Fonts, and Other Preferences in Vim

Customization is one of the pillars of Vim's popularity. It enables users to tailor their editing environment to their liking, making coding or writing more efficient and enjoyable. In this section, we will delve into the various customization options Vim offers, from aesthetic changes like colors and fonts to functional preferences that alter the editor's behavior.

**Changing Color Schemes**

Vim's appearance can be dramatically altered through color schemes, which are sets of instructions defining the colors of the Vim interface.

- **Applying Color Schemes**: To change the color scheme, use the command `:colorscheme [scheme]`, replacing `[scheme]` with the name of the desired color scheme.

- **Finding Schemes**: Vim comes with several pre-installed color schemes, and many more can be downloaded from repositories or Vim plugin managers.

**Customizing Fonts**

In Vim's GUI version, GVim, you can specify the font style and size.

- **Setting Fonts**: Use the command `:set guifont=[font]:h[size]`, where `[font]` is the font name and `[size]` is the size in points.
- **Example**: `:set guifont=Monaco:h12` sets the font to Monaco with a size of 12 points.

**Adjusting Syntax Highlighting**

Syntax highlighting makes code easier to read by coloring text according to its syntactic structure.

- **Enabling/Disabling**: Toggle syntax highlighting with `:syntax on` or `:syntax off`.
- **Customizing**: Modify the syntax files in the `~/.vim/syntax/` directory for finer control over the colors used for different syntax elements.

## Modifying Preferences

Vim's functionality can also be customized through a set of preferences.

- **Line Numbering**: Choose between absolute line numbers (`:set number`), relative line numbers (`:set relativenumber`), or disable them (`:set nonumber`).

- **Tabs and Spaces**: Configure tab behavior with commands like `:set tabstop=4` and `:set expandtab` to convert tabs to spaces.

- **Search Behavior**: Control search features with commands like `:set ignorecase` and `:set hlsearch` for case-insensitive searches and highlighting search results.

## Saving Customizations

After you've decided on your preferred settings:

- **Persistent Configuration**: Add your custom settings to the `.vimrc` file to make them persist across Vim sessions.

- **Reloading Settings**: After modifying `.vimrc`, reload the settings without restarting Vim by running `:source ~/.vimrc`.

**Summary**

Customizing Vim to your preferences not only personalizes your editing experience but can also lead to more productive sessions. Whether you're adjusting visual aspects like colors and fonts or tweaking functional behaviors through Vim's settings, the power of Vim lies in its adaptability to the user's needs. Take the time to explore and experiment with Vim's vast customization capabilities, and you will find that Vim can become an indispensable tool in your software development toolkit.

# 4.5 Lab - Changing Configuration Settings for the Vim Editor

**Introduction:**

Customizing your Vim configuration settings can greatly enhance your editing experience. In this lab, you'll learn how to change various settings in the Vim editor to match your preferences. We'll cover essential settings like enabling line numbering, adjusting tab stops, and enabling autoindent.

**Objectives:**

- Learn how to change and customize Vim configuration settings.
- Enable line numbering for better code navigation.
- Adjust tab stops to control indentation behavior.
- Enable autoindent to maintain consistent code formatting.

**Before You Begin:**
Ensure that you have Vim installed on your system.

**Instructions:**

### Step 1: Open a File in Vim

1. Open your terminal.
2. Navigate to the directory containing a text file you want to edit with Vim.
3. Launch Vim and open a file by typing `vim filename.txt` and press Enter.

### Step 2: Enable Line Numbering

1. In Normal mode, press `Esc` to ensure you're in the command mode.
2. Enter the following command to enable line numbering: `:set number`
3. Press Enter. You should now see line numbers on the left side of the screen.

### Step 3: Adjust Tab Stops

1. In Normal mode, press `Esc` to ensure you're in the command mode.
2. Enter the following command to set the number of spaces for a tab stop (e.g., 4 spaces): `:set tabstop=4`
3. Press Enter. This sets the tab width to 4 spaces.

## Step 4: Enable Autoindent

1. In Normal mode, press `Esc` to ensure you're in the command mode.

2. Enter the following command to enable autoindent: `:set autoindent`

3. Press Enter. This will automatically indent new lines to match the previous line's indentation.

## Step 5: Save Your Changes

1. In Normal mode, press `Esc` to ensure you're in the command mode.

2. Save your changes by typing `:w` and pressing Enter.

## Step 6: Exit Vim

1. In Normal mode, press `Esc` to ensure you're in the command mode.

2. To exit Vim, type `:q` and press Enter.

## Summary:

In this lab, you've learned how to change configuration settings in the Vim editor. You enabled line numbering for better navigation, adjusted tab stops to control indentation, and enabled autoindent to maintain consistent code formatting. Customizing Vim settings can significantly improve your editing experience and productivity.

# 4.6 Vim Plugins

Vim, in its vanilla state, is a powerful tool, but its true potential is unleashed through the use of plugins. Plugins extend Vim's functionality far beyond basic text editing, catering to a vast array of needs from syntax highlighting to file management and code completion. This section will provide insights into how to enhance your Vim experience by installing and managing plugins.

**Finding Vim Plugins**

Before installation, you need to find plugins that suit your needs. Websites like Vim Awesome are excellent resources, offering a wide array of community-vetted plugins.

**Plugin Managers**

While it's possible to install plugins manually, using a plugin manager simplifies the process. Popular plugin managers include:

- **Vim-Plug**: Lightweight and provides on-demand plugin loading.
- **Pathogen**: One of the first plugin managers that turned each plugin into a 'bundle'.
- **Vundle**: Offers easy installation and management with a Git-based workflow.

## Installing a Plugin Manager

Here's a quick guide on installing Vim-Plug:

### Download Vim-Plug:

```
curl -fLo ~/.vim/autoload/plug.vim --create-dirs \
  https://raw.githubusercontent.com/junegunn/vim-
plug/master/plug.vim
```

**Configure `.vimrc`**: Add the following to your `.vimrc` file to initialize Vim-Plug:

```
call plug#begin('~/.vim/plugged')

" Place your plugin installations here, e.g.:
" Plug 'preservim/nerdtree'

call plug#end()
```

**Install Plugins**: Restart Vim, and run `:PlugInstall` to install the plugins you've listed.

### Using Plugins

Once installed, plugins may require additional steps to fully integrate with your workflow:

- **Configuration**: Some plugins have settings that can be customized in your `.vimrc` file.

- **Key Bindings**: Set key bindings to easily access plugin functionality.

- **Dependencies**: Ensure all dependencies are met, as some plugins might depend on external tools or other Vim plugins.

### Keeping Plugins Updated

Keep your plugins up to date to benefit from the latest features and bug fixes:

- **Updating**: Use your plugin manager's commands to update, such as `:PlugUpdate` with Vim-Plug.

- **Review Changes**: It's a good practice to review the changelog or commit messages for updates, especially for plugins that are critical to your workflow.

**Troubleshooting Plugins**

Encountering issues with plugins can be common:

- **Conflicts**: Disable other plugins to isolate conflicts.

- **Documentation**: Refer to the plugin's documentation for troubleshooting tips.

- **Community Support**: Use community forums or GitHub issues to seek help.

**Summary**

Plugins are a cornerstone of Vim's adaptability and one of the main reasons for its enduring popularity among developers. By effectively utilizing plugins, you can tailor Vim to your exact specifications, turning a robust text editor into a personalized integrated development environment. The process of finding, installing, and maintaining plugins is made easier with the use of a plugin manager, and with the right set of plugins, there are few limits to what Vim can do.

# Chapter 5 - Macros in Vim

# 5.1 Vim Macros

In the realm of text editing, efficiency is key. Vim macros are one of the most potent tools in Vim's arsenal, enabling users to record a sequence of commands and play them back to automate repetitive tasks. This feature can drastically reduce the time spent on mundane editing tasks. This chapter will cover the basics of recording and using macros in Vim.

### Understanding Vim Macros

Macros in Vim are essentially recordings of keystrokes that can be played back to automate complex or repetitive tasks.

- **Recording a Macro**: To record a macro, you press q followed by a letter to name the macro (e.g., qa to record a macro named 'a').

- **Performing Actions**: After starting the recording, you perform the series of actions you want to automate.

- **Stopping the Recording**: You press q again to stop and save the recording.

## Using Macros

Once a macro is recorded, it can be played back any number of times.

- **Playing Back a Macro**: Press @ followed by the macro name (e.g., @a to play back macro 'a').

- **Repeating Macros**: You can repeat a macro multiple times by prefixing the playback command with a number (e.g., 10@a to play the macro 'a' ten times).

- **Combining Macros**: Macros can be combined by playing one macro within the recording of another.

## Advanced Macro Usage

Macros can be used for complex text manipulations and can even include conditional logic.

- **Editing within Macros**: You can insert, delete, copy, and perform more complex editing actions within a macro.

- **Nested Macros**: Macros can call other macros, allowing for modular and complex automations.

**Saving Macros**

Vim macros are temporary by default, but you can save them for later use.

- **Saving to Vimrc**: You can save macro recordings in your `.vimrc` file for persistence across sessions by mapping them to keys.

- **Storing in Registers**: Vim macros are stored in registers, which means they can be written to and read from files if needed.

**Troubleshooting Macros**

Sometimes macros don't work as expected on playback.

- **Syntax Errors**: Ensure that commands within the macro are correct and would work if executed individually.

- **Context Sensitivity**: Macros may behave differently depending on the context, such as cursor position or text selection.

## Summary

Macros are an incredibly powerful feature that can transform the Vim experience. By learning to record, play back, and manage macros, you can automate a wide range of tasks, from simple to complex. This chapter has introduced the basic concepts and commands to start using macros effectively in Vim. As you practice these skills, you'll find that macros can significantly enhance your productivity and accuracy in text editing.

# 5.2 Lab Vim Macros

**Introduction**

Macros in Vim are a game-changer for anyone looking to boost their productivity. They can turn repetitive tasks into a single keystroke operation, ensuring consistency and efficiency. This lab session is designed to guide you through creating and using macros in Vim, from the simplest to more complex sequences. By the end, you will be able to automate repetitive editing tasks with ease.

**Objectives**

- Learn how to record and play a simple macro in Vim.
- Understand how to construct a macro for more complex tasks.
- Practice using macros to perform repetitive edits quickly.

### Exercise 1: Recording a Simple Macro

1. **Objective**: Record a macro that adds a semicolon at the end of a line.

2. **Task**: Open Vim and type out a few lines of text that mimic code lines missing semicolons.

3. **Action**:

    - Move the cursor to the first line.
    - Press q followed by a to start recording the macro to register 'a'.
    - Press $ to go to the end of the line.
    - Type ; to insert the semicolon.
    - Press j to move down to the next line (to prepare for repeated actions).
    - Press q to stop recording the macro.

### Exercise 2: Playing Back a Simple Macro

1. **Objective**: Play back the recorded macro to add semicolons to all lines.

2. **Task**: Use the macro recorded in Exercise 1 on the remaining lines.

3. **Action**:

    - Press @a to play back the macro on the next line.
    - Type 2@a to apply the macro to the next two lines, or use @@ to replay the last used macro.

**Exercise 3: Recording a Complex Macro**

1. **Objective**: Record a macro that formats a block of text as a comment.

2. **Task**: Write a paragraph of text that you want to comment out.

3. **Action**:

   - Move the cursor to the beginning of the paragraph.

   - Press q followed by b to start recording the macro to register 'b'.

   - Press I to insert at the beginning of the line and type // to denote a comment.

   - Press Esc to return to Normal Mode, then j to move to the next line, and ^ to move to the first non-blank character of the line.

   - Press q to stop recording the macro.

**Exercise 4: Using a Complex Macro**

1. **Objective**: Use the complex macro to comment out multiple lines of text.

2. **Task**: Apply the recorded macro to a block of text.

3. **Action**:

   - Press @b to apply the comment formatting to the next line.

   - Repeat the macro as many times as needed to comment out the entire paragraph.

**Summary**

Through these exercises, you have practiced creating and using macros in Vim, which can drastically streamline your editing process. Starting with a basic macro to append a character to each line, you progressed to a more complex macro designed to format blocks of text. Macros can be particularly powerful when dealing with repetitive tasks across large files. With the skills acquired in this lab, you're well on your way to becoming a more efficient and productive Vim user. Remember, the true power of macros lies in their ability to be customized to fit any sequence of commands you find yourself repeating.

# 5.3 Recording and Playing Back Macros

Macros in Vim are not just a feature; they're a productivity force-multiplier. They serve as an automated assistant, taking on the repetitive tasks that can bog down the editing process. This chapter will guide you through the steps to effectively record and play back macros in Vim, providing you with a valuable tool to amplify your text-editing prowess.

**The Basics of Vim Macros**

A macro is essentially a recording of a series of commands that you can execute at a later time. These commands can perform almost any task you can do manually in Vim, from inserting or deleting text to complex code refactoring.

**Recording a Macro**

1. **Start the Recording**: Press q followed by a register key (a-z or A-Z) where the macro will be stored. For example, qa starts recording a macro in the 'a' register.

2. **Perform the Commands**: Carry out the sequence of commands you want to automate. This can be anything from simple text insertion to a series of commands across lines.

3. **Stop the Recording**: Press q again to end the recording.

**Playing Back a Macro**

- **Single Playback**: Press @ followed by the register key to play back the macro once. For example, @a plays back the macro stored in the 'a' register.

- **Repeated Playback**: To play a macro multiple times, type a number before the playback command, like 10@a to play the macro ten times.

**Complex Macros**

Vim allows for the recording of very complex series of commands. You can:

- **Include Movement Commands**: Use commands like j to move down a line or w to move to the next word.

- **Work Across Lines**: Combine movement commands with editing commands to make changes across multiple lines.

- **Combine Macros**: Execute one macro from within another for more complex automation.

## Editing Macros

If you make a mistake while recording a macro, you don't have to start over. Instead, you can:

- **Update a Macro**: By re-recording it using the same register.
- **Edit a Macro**: Since macros are stored in registers, you can edit them by pasting the macro content into the document, making changes, and yanking it back into the register.

## Saving Macros

Macros are stored in registers only for the current session by default. To save a macro for future use:

- **Save in vimrc**: Add a line to your `.vimrc` file using the `let` command to save the macro to a register.

## Troubleshooting Macros

If a macro doesn't work as expected, check the following:

- **Correct Mode**: Ensure you are in the correct mode when starting and ending the macro.
- **Unintended Commands**: Avoid extraneous keystrokes during recording; they will be part of the macro.

## Summary

Macros are a testament to Vim's flexibility and power. They can significantly reduce the time spent on repetitive tasks, allowing you to focus on the creative aspects of your work. By understanding how to record, play back, and manage macros, you can harness Vim's full potential and elevate your text editing to new heights of efficiency and effectiveness. As with many Vim features, practice is key— experiment with macros, and soon they will become an integral part of your Vim toolkit.

# 5.4 Using Macros for Repetitive Tasks

One of Vim's most powerful features is its ability to automate repetitive tasks using macros. This not only saves time but also ensures accuracy and consistency in your work. Macros can be simple, such as adding the same text to the end of every line, or complex, involving conditional statements and multiple commands. This chapter will introduce the concept of using Vim macros for repetitive tasks and provide examples of common macros.

### Creating Macros for Common Repetitive Tasks

The real power of macros lies in their ability to turn a series of actions into a single command. Here are a few examples of how macros can be used:

### Example 1: Formatting a List

- **Task**: You have a list of items that you want to format with Markdown list syntax.

- **Macro**:
    - Start recording with qa.
    - Move to the start of the line with ^.
    - Insert the list syntax with i- (dash followed by space).
    - Move to the next line with j.
    - Stop recording with q.
    - Use @a to apply this macro to each line in your list.

## Example 2: Refactoring Variable Names

- **Task**: You need to refactor a variable name across multiple lines of code.

- **Macro**:
  - Start recording with qb.
  - Search for the variable name with /
    oldVarName.
  - Enter substitute command with :s//
    newVarName/ (leaving the search pattern
    empty reuses the last search).
  - Navigate to the next instance with n.
  - Stop recording with q.
  - Execute the macro with @b and repeat
    as necessary.

100

## Example 3: Code Cleanup

- **Task**: Remove trailing whitespace from the end of each line in a file.

- **Macro**:
    - Start recording with qc.
    - Move to the start of the line with ^.
    - Search for trailing whitespace with / \+ $.
    - Substitute the found whitespace with :s///.
    - Move to the next line with j.
    - Stop recording with q.
    - Use @c to clean up each line.

## Tips for Efficient Macro Usage

- **Plan Your Steps**: Before recording, plan out the exact keystrokes needed to avoid errors.

- **Use Relative Movements**: Use commands like j (down) and ^ (beginning of line) to make your macro work regardless of the starting position.

- **Check Your Registers**: Use :reg to see what's stored in your registers and ensure you're not overwriting an important macro.

**Saving Macros for Long-Term Use**

While macros are usually temporary, you can save them for repeated use:

- **Save in vimrc**: Assign a macro to a shortcut key in your `.vimrc` file for easy access.
- **Write to a File**: Save your macro by yanking it into a buffer and writing that buffer to a file.

**Summary**

Macros are among the most efficient tools in Vim for dealing with repetitive tasks. By learning to record, edit, and apply macros, you can significantly speed up your workflow and reduce the potential for human error. This chapter has provided examples of macros that can be used for common tasks, but the possibilities are nearly endless. With practice, you will find new ways to use macros to suit your specific needs, making Vim an even more powerful tool in your software development arsenal.

# 5.5 Quiz - Macros in Vim

1) What is a macro in Vim?

     A. A sequence of keystrokes recorded and saved for later use

     B. A plugin used for syntax highlighting

     C. A command to create a new file in Vim

     D. A command to close Vim

2) How can a user start recording a macro in Vim?

     A. Pressing the "q" key followed by a letter to name the macro

     B. Pressing the "r" key to start recording

     C. Pressing the "i" key to enter insert mode

     D. Pressing the "Esc" key to enter command mode

3) How can a user replay a macro in Vim?

     A. Pressing the "q" key followed by the letter name of the macro

     B. Pressing the "r" key to start recording

     C. Pressing the "i" key to enter insert mode

     D. Pressing the "Esc" key to enter command mode

4) What is the purpose of using macros in Vim?

     A. To automate repetitive tasks

     B. To change the syntax highlighting of a file

     C. To navigate between files in Vim

     D. To customize the Vim interface

5) How can a user save a macro in Vim to use it in other sessions?

    A. By copying and pasting the macro code to a separate file

    B. By saving the macro to the .vimrc file

    C. By saving the macro to a separate file and sourcing it in Vim

    D. By typing the macro code every time it is needed

# Chapter 6 - Using Vim for Coding

# 6.1 Syntax Highlighting

Syntax highlighting is an essential feature in modern text editors that improves readability and comprehension of code. In Vim, syntax highlighting can dramatically enhance the user experience by visually distinguishing keywords, variables, operators, and other syntax elements. This not only aids in code understanding but also helps in detecting syntax errors.

**Enabling Syntax Highlighting**

To turn on syntax highlighting in Vim, you'll need to enter Command Mode. Here's how you can enable it:

1. Open Vim.
2. Press `Esc` to ensure you are in Normal Mode.
3. Enter Command Mode by typing `:`.
4. Type `syntax on` and press `Enter`.

Vim will then enable syntax highlighting for the file type it detects based on the file extension. If Vim does not automatically recognize the file type, you can set it manually with the `:set filetype=<type>` command, where `<type>` is the file type like `html`, `python`, `javascript`, etc.

## Customizing Syntax Highlighting

Vim allows you to customize syntax highlighting to suit your preferences:

- **Change Color Scheme**: Change the color scheme with `:colorscheme <name>`, where <name> is the name of the scheme you want to use.

- **Customize Specific Syntax**: Use `:highlight` to set the colors for specific syntax groups. For example, `:highlight Comment ctermfg=green` would change the color of comments to green in a terminal with color support.

- **Enable Filetype Plugins**: To get the most out of syntax highlighting, enable filetype plugins with `:filetype plugin on`.

### Troubleshooting Syntax Highlighting

If syntax highlighting is not working as expected, consider the following troubleshooting steps:

- **Check Vim Version**: Ensure you are using a version of Vim that supports syntax highlighting, typically Vim 6.0 and above.

- **Verify Filetype Detection**: Confirm that Vim is detecting the correct filetype with `:set filetype?`.

- **Inspect Vim Configuration**: Look at your `.vimrc` file for any settings that might be affecting syntax highlighting.

### Summary

Syntax highlighting in Vim is not just about aesthetics; it serves a practical purpose in making code more readable and understandable. By enabling and customizing syntax highlighting, you can create a more visually organized and pleasing coding environment that caters to your workflow. Remember that Vim's powerful customization options allow you to tailor the editor to your exact needs, and with proper configuration, you can ensure that syntax highlighting works seamlessly for a wide range of programming languages and file types.

## 6.2 Using Vim for Coding Tasks

Vim is not just a text editor; it's a preferred tool for many programmers due to its powerful features designed to facilitate coding tasks. It supports a wide range of programming languages and provides features such as auto-indentation, syntax highlighting, commenting, and code folding, which are essential for efficient code writing and editing. In this chapter, we will delve into these features and provide guidance on how to use them effectively.

### Auto-Indentation

Indentation is crucial in programming for readability and structure. Vim offers auto-indentation to maintain consistent spacing.

- **Setting Indentation**: Use `:set autoindent` to turn on auto-indentation, which carries over the indentation from the previous line.

- **Smart Indentation**: For languages like C or Java, `:set smartindent` or `:set cindent` offers language-specific indentation.

- **Adjusting Indent Size**: Set the number of spaces for an indent with `:set shiftwidth=4` and the size of a Tab with `:set tabstop=4`.

## Commenting

Commenting is a routine part of coding, and Vim can streamline the process.

- **Single-Line Commenting**: Comment out a line by inserting the appropriate comment symbol (like // for C++ or # for Python) at the start of the line.

- **Block Commenting**: Use visual block mode by pressing Ctrl-V, select the lines you want to comment, and then use I to insert the comment symbol at the start of each line.

## Code Folding

Folding allows you to hide sections of code to get a clearer view of what you're working on.

- **Creating a Fold**: Select the lines you want to fold with visual mode (v), then press zf to create the fold.

- **Navigating Folds**: Use za to toggle a fold open or closed, zM to close all folds, and zR to open all folds.

110

### Using Plugins for Enhanced Functionality

While Vim's native features are powerful, plugins can enhance the coding experience.

- **Plugin Management**: Tools like Vim-Plug or Pathogen can be used to manage plugins.
- **Popular Plugins**: Plugins such as NERDTree for directory exploration or YouCompleteMe for code completion can be extremely beneficial.

### Integrating Version Control

Version control systems like Git can be integrated directly into Vim.

- **Vim-fugitive**: This is a popular plugin that allows you to run Git commands within Vim.
- **Viewing Differences**: Use `:Gdiff` to view changes in the context of your current working directory.

## Summary

Vim's efficiency and customizability make it an excellent choice for coding. With features like indentation, commenting, and code folding, Vim streamlines the coding process, allowing developers to focus on writing high-quality code. Additionally, the extensive ecosystem of plugins further extends Vim's capabilities, enabling functionalities that rival modern IDEs. Whether you're writing a quick script or working on a large project, Vim provides the tools necessary to accomplish your coding tasks with precision and speed.

## 6.3 Understanding Vim Integration with Different Programming Languages

Vim, while being a text editor at its core, offers extensive support for programming across various languages. Its flexibility and adaptability stem from powerful built-in features and a vast ecosystem of plugins and scripts. This chapter will delve into how Vim integrates with different programming languages and how to optimize Vim for a seamless coding experience.

**Built-in Language Support**

Vim comes preloaded with support for numerous programming languages, providing syntax highlighting, indentation rules, and other language-specific features.

- **Syntax Files**: Vim uses syntax files to define the coloring and styling of different language elements. These are typically located in the `/syntax/` directory of Vim's runtime path.

- **Filetype Detection**: Vim automatically detects the filetype based on the file extension and applies the appropriate syntax rules.

- **Language-Specific Settings**: For certain languages, Vim includes compiler settings, allowing you to compile code directly from within the editor using `:make`.

### Customizing Vim for Programming Languages

- **Setting Filetype**: Manually set the filetype if Vim does not recognize it with `:set filetype=python` for Python, for example.

- **Indentation**: Customize indentation according to language standards with `:set shiftwidth=2` for languages like Ruby or `:set expandtab` to use spaces instead of tabs.

### Language-Specific Plugins

For more advanced language integration, Vim can be extended with plugins.

- **Autocompletion**: Plugins like YouCompleteMe provide intelligent code completion for various languages.

- **Linting**: Syntastic or ALE can be used for on-the-fly linting, providing syntax checking and style recommendations.

- **Language Servers**: Integration with Language Server Protocol (LSP) via plugins like CoC (Conquer of Completion) or vim-lsp allows Vim to provide features like go-to definition, symbol renaming, and more.

### Integrating Build Tools and Environments

- **Task Runners**: Plugins like vim-dispatch can integrate with build tools and task runners, allowing you to run tasks without leaving Vim.

- **Debuggers**: Vim can interface with debuggers for languages like Python (through pdb) and JavaScript (using Chrome DevTools) using plugins or Vim's terminal feature.

### Managing Dependencies and Projects

- **Dependency Management**: For languages with dependency management tools like npm for JavaScript or pip for Python, Vim can execute these tools via its command-line mode.

- **Project Navigation**: Use plugins like NERDTree for directory exploration and file navigation within a project.

### Summary

Vim's inherent support for a wide range of programming languages makes it a versatile editor for developers. By leveraging built-in functionalities, custom settings, and a rich selection of plugins, Vim can be turned into a powerful environment tailored for different programming languages. The editor's ability to integrate with build systems, debuggers, and other development tools further enhances its role in the modern programming workflow. With Vim's deep customization possibilities, each developer can craft their unique development environment that aligns with their needs and preferences.

## 6.4 Quiz - Using Vim for Coding

1) What command can be used to automatically indent a block of code in Vim?
   A. "V"
   B. ">"
   C. "gcc"
   D. "zf}"

2) How can Vim automatically add a comment to a line of code?
   A. "V"
   B. ">"
   C. "gcc"
   D. "zf}"

3) Which command can be used to fold a section of code in Vim?
   A. "V"
   B. ">"
   C. "gcc"
   D. "zf}"
   Answer: D

4) How can Vim be customized to automatically indent code based on user preferences?
  A. By using plugins
  B. By using the ">>" command
  C. By using the "gcc" command
  D. By modifying the .vimrc file


5) What is the purpose of code folding in Vim?
  A. To save disk space
  B. To improve code readability
  C. To increase program performance
  D. To remove unnecessary code

# Module 7 - Troubleshooting Vim

# 7.1 Common Issues When Using the Vim Editor

The Vim editor, while powerful, comes with a steep learning curve, and users often encounter a range of common issues. This section will outline some of the frequent challenges faced by Vim users, from beginners to those with more experience. Understanding these issues can help in troubleshooting and streamlining your editing process in Vim.

**Issue 1: Accidental Insertion of Commands**

Users often find themselves typing commands while still in Normal Mode, which leads to unintended insertions or alterations in the text.

- **Resolution**: Always ensure you're in Insert Mode (by pressing i) before you start typing text.

**Issue 2: Difficulty Exiting Vim**

New users frequently struggle with exiting Vim properly.

- **Resolution**: Type :q to quit (if no changes were made), or :wq to write changes and quit, and :q! to quit without saving changes.

**Issue 3: Lost Text Due to Unintended Undo**

Pressing u in Normal Mode undoes the last change, which can lead to accidental loss of text if pressed unintentionally.

- **Resolution**: Use the redo command Ctrl-R to recover the lost text.

**Issue 4: Confusion Over Modes**

Vim's modal interface can confuse users, particularly those accustomed to non-modal editors.

- **Resolution**: Practice the habit of hitting Esc to go back to Normal Mode, which is a safe default for deciding the next action.

**Issue 5: Search Patterns Not Found**

When searches return "Pattern not found," it could be due to case sensitivity or complex patterns.

- **Resolution**: Use :set ignorecase for case-insensitive searches or refine your search pattern for accuracy.

## Issue 6: Problems with Copy-Paste From External Sources

Pasting from an external source can introduce unexpected formatting or characters.

- **Resolution**: Use Vim's paste mode by typing `:set paste` before pasting from an external source.

## Issue 7: Files Not Saving

Beginners often encounter issues when trying to save files, receiving "Permission denied" or similar errors.

- **Resolution**: Ensure you have write permissions for the file and directory. Save with elevated privileges using `:w !sudo tee %` if necessary.

## Issue 8: Plugin or Configuration Errors

Custom plugins and configurations can cause errors or unexpected behavior.

- **Resolution**: Review your `.vimrc` file for errors, and disable plugins one by one to isolate the issue.

**Summary**

Working with Vim involves a learning process where encountering and resolving common issues is a part of the journey to mastery. From learning to navigate Vim's modes effectively to dealing with configuration challenges, each issue resolved reinforces your understanding of Vim's environment. By becoming familiar with these common pitfalls and their solutions, you can minimize frustration and make your time with Vim more productive and enjoyable. Remember, practice and patience are key components in becoming proficient with Vim.

## 7.2 Troubleshooting Tips and Tricks

Vim, with its robust features, can sometimes present challenges even to experienced users. Encountering issues is a natural part of the learning curve. This chapter provides practical troubleshooting tips and tricks to help you overcome common hurdles, ensuring a smoother Vim experience.

**Tip 1: Undoing Accidental Changes**

If you've made changes accidentally, Vim's undo feature is your first line of defense. However, if u isn't enough:

- Use `:earlier 10m` to revert the file to the state it was in 10 minutes earlier.
- For more granular control, use the undo tree with `:undolist`.

**Tip 2: Resolving Cursor Movement Issues**

When cursor movement isn't behaving as expected:

- Check if you're in Insert or Replace mode and return to Normal Mode with `Esc`.
- If using a plugin for movement, consult the plugin documentation for conflicts or issues.

### Tip 3: Fixing Syntax Highlighting

Syntax highlighting can sometimes go awry, especially with large files or after pasting text.

- Refresh the syntax highlighting with `:syntax sync fromstart` or `:syntax off` followed by `:syntax on`.

### Tip 4: Dealing with Slow Performance

Vim is generally fast, but performance can lag due to:

- Large files: Use `:set lazyredraw` to make Vim less eager to redraw the screen.
- Complex regex: Simplify your search patterns or use `:set regexpengine=1` to switch to the older, faster regex engine.

### Tip 5: Managing Plugins

Plugins can enhance Vim but also cause unexpected behavior.

- Use `:scriptnames` to see which scripts are loaded.
- Temporarily disable all plugins by starting Vim with `vim --noplugin` and then re-enable them one by one.

**Tip 6: Copy-Pasting Without Auto-Indenting Issues**

Pasting text sometimes triggers auto-indenting, resulting in misaligned code.

- Before pasting, enable paste mode with `:set paste`, and after pasting, disable it with `:set nopaste`.

**Tip 7: Searching for Text Efficiently**

Inefficient searches can lead to frustration.

- Use `:set incsearch` to see matches as you type.
- Use `:set hlsearch` to highlight matches and `:nohlsearch` to turn off the highlighting.

**Tip 8: Editing Files with Root Privileges**

Trying to save changes to a file without sufficient permissions is a common issue.

- Save changes with `:w !sudo tee %` to write to a file with root privileges.

**Tip 9: Handling Line Endings Across Different Operating Systems**

Inconsistent line endings can cause problems when moving files between Windows and Unix systems.

- Convert line endings with `:set fileformat=unix` or `:set fileformat=dos`.

**Tip 10: Restoring Vim to Default Settings**

When all else fails, or Vim is acting unpredictably:

- Revert to the default settings with `:runtime defaults.vim`.

- Check your `.vimrc` for any problematic configurations by commenting out sections and testing.

**Summary**

Vim's complexity can occasionally lead to issues, but with the right troubleshooting tips and tricks, you can resolve most problems efficiently. Understanding how to undo changes, manage cursor movement, handle syntax highlighting, deal with slow performance, manage plugins, and work with different file permissions will equip you to address the majority of challenges you might face. Remember, troubleshooting is an iterative process; patience and a methodical approach will often lead you to a solution.

# 7.3 Understanding Error Messages and How to Fix Them

Error messages in Vim are not merely interruptions—they are signposts pointing towards resolution. Understanding these messages is crucial to maintaining a seamless editing workflow. This chapter will focus on deciphering common Vim error messages and provide guidance on resolving the issues they indicate.

**Common Error Messages**

## 1. "E37: No write since last change (add ! to override)"

- **Meaning**: Vim is warning you that there are unsaved changes in the buffer.

- **Fix**: Save the changes with `:w` before exiting or force quit without saving with `:q!`.

## 2. "E486: Pattern not found: [pattern]"

- **Meaning**: The search term you entered cannot be found in the text.

- **Fix**: Check the search term for typos or adjust it for accuracy. Consider using `:set ignorecase` for a case-insensitive search.

## 3. "E32: No file name"

- **Meaning**: This occurs when trying to save a file that was not opened with a name.

- **Fix**: Provide a name for the new file using `:saveas [file_name]`.

### 4. "E305: No alternate file"

- **Meaning**: Vim keeps track of the "alternate file", which is typically the last file you had open. This error occurs when trying to switch to an alternate file that doesn't exist.
- **Fix**: Open or create a new file to establish it as the alternate file.

### 5. "E488: Trailing characters"

- **Meaning**: Vim commands need to be exact, and this error indicates there are unexpected characters after a command.
- **Fix**: Reread the command you entered for any extraneous characters and re-enter it correctly.

### 6. "E95: Buffer [number] exists"

- **Meaning**: You're trying to open a file in a new buffer that is already open in another buffer.
- **Fix**: Use `:buffer [number]` to switch to the buffer where the file is already open or close the existing buffer first.

### 7. "E325: ATTENTION Found a swap file by the name..."

- **Meaning**: Vim creates a swap file for unsaved changes if it crashes or if another instance of Vim is editing the same file.
- **Fix**: If the other instance is still running, close it properly. If Vim had crashed, recover the changes from the swap file or delete it if it's no longer needed.

## 8. "E518: Unknown option: [option]"

- **Meaning**: Vim does not recognize an option, possibly due to a typo or a misconfiguration in `.vimrc`.

- **Fix**: Check the spelling of the option and consult Vim documentation or help files for valid options.

## 9. "E676: Invalid option argument: [argument]"

- **Meaning**: The argument provided to a Vim option is not valid.

- **Fix**: Look up the option in Vim's help (`:help [option]`) to find valid arguments.

## 10. "E212: Can't open file for writing"

- **Meaning**: Vim is unable to write to the file, typically due to permission issues.

- **Fix**: Ensure you have write permissions for the file, or save it in a directory where you do have permissions.

## Summary

Vim's error messages, while sometimes cryptic, are there to help you navigate the complexities of the editor. By understanding these messages and knowing the common fixes, you can quickly address issues without interrupting your editing flow. Most errors stem from simple mistakes or overlooks, and they can often be resolved with a few keystrokes. When in doubt, Vim's extensive help system (`:help`) is an invaluable resource for troubleshooting and learning. As you grow more familiar with these messages and their remedies, you'll find that they become less of a stumbling block and more of a guide towards becoming an adept Vim user.

# Chapter 8 Summary

## 8.1 Course Summary

In this course, we have explored the Vim editor and how it can be used to edit and manage text files efficiently and effectively. We have covered various topics such as launching and exiting Vim, installing and using plugins, customizing preferences, understanding the .vimrc file, and using macros for repetitive tasks. We have also discussed common issues that users may encounter when using Vim and how to solve them.

By completing this course, you should have a solid understanding of the Vim editor and its features. With practice, you can become proficient in using Vim to edit and manage text files more efficiently and effectively. Thank you for attending this course. We hope that you have found it informative and helpful. If you have any questions or feedback, please do not hesitate to contact us. We wish you all the best in your Vim editing journey!

## 8.2 About the Author

**Eric Frick**

I have worked in software development and IT operations
for 30 years. I have worked as a Software Developer,
Software Development Manager, Software Architect, and
as an Operations Manager. Also, for the last five years, I
have taught evening classes on various IT related subjects
at several local universities. I currently work as a Cloud
Instructor for Mirantis Inc. (https://mirantis.com),
developing cloud-based certification courses. In 2015, I
founded destinlearning.com, and I am developing a series
of books and courses that can provide practical information
to students on various IT and software development topics.

If you would like to connect with me on LinkedIn, here is the link to my profile:

https://www.linkedin.com/in/efrick/

Also, if you have any questions or comments about this book you can contact me directly at:

sales@destinlearning.com

## 8.3 More From Destin Learning

Thank you so much for your interest in this book. I hope it has given you a good start in the exciting field of Information Technology. If you would like to learn more about software development, you can check out my book, The Beginner's Guide to C#. You can learn more by clicking on the link below.

https://courses.destinlearning.com

# Appendix A - Answers to Quiz Questions

## A.1 Quiz – Advanced Editing

**Question 1**
What is the command to replace all occurrences of the word "apple" with "orange" in the entire file?

A) `:s/apple/orange/g`
B) `:%s/apple/orange/`
C) `:%s/apple/orange/g`
D) `:g/apple/orange/`

**Correct Answer**: C) `:%s/apple/orange/g`

**Question 2**
How do you join the current line and the next three lines into one in Vim?

A) `3J`
B) `J3`
C) `jjjJ`
D) `Jjjj`

**Correct Answer**: A) `3J`

## Question 3
If you wanted to change the case of the entire line to uppercase, which command would you use?

A) gUU
B) guu
C) gUgU
D) ggU

**Correct Answer**: A) gUU

## Question 4
To record a macro in Vim, which key do you press first?

A) m
B) r
C) q
D) a

**Correct Answer**: C) q

## Question 5
Which command would you use to return to a previously marked position labeled 'k'?

A) mk
B) bk
C) 'k
D) goto k

**Correct Answer**: C) 'k

## Question 6

What is the command to replace the word "Vim" with "VIM" only on lines that contain the word "editor"?

A) `:%s/editor.*Vim/VIM/g`
B) `:g/editor/s/Vim/VIM/`
C) `:%g/editor/s/Vim/VIM/`
D) `:g/editor/s/Vim/VIM/g`

**Correct Answer**: D) `:g/editor/s/Vim/VIM/g`

## Question 7

How do you move to the beginning of the next paragraph in Vim?

A) `}`
B) `{{`
C) `[[`
D) `{`

**Correct Answer**: A) `}`

## Question 8

If you have multiple files open in Vim, how do you list all the open buffers?

A) `:ls`
B) `:buffers`
C) `:open`
D) Both A and B

**Correct Answer**: D) Both A and B

## Summary

This short quiz is designed to test your knowledge of advanced Vim commands after completing the lab section. Understanding these commands is crucial for efficient navigation and editing in Vim. Regular practice of these commands will reinforce your memory, making your interaction with Vim more effective and intuitive.

# A.2 Quiz - Macros in Vim

1) What is a macro in Vim?

    A. A sequence of keystrokes recorded and saved for later use

    B. A plugin used for syntax highlighting

    C. A command to create a new file in Vim

    D. A command to close Vim

    Answer: A

2) How can a user start recording a macro in Vim?

    A. Pressing the "q" key followed by a letter to name the macro

    B. Pressing the "r" key to start recording

    C. Pressing the "i" key to enter insert mode

    D. Pressing the "Esc" key to enter command mode

    Answer: A

3) How can a user replay a macro in Vim?

    A. Pressing the "q" key followed by the letter name of the macro

    B. Pressing the "r" key to start recording

    C. Pressing the "i" key to enter insert mode

    D. Pressing the "Esc" key to enter command mode

    Answer: A

4) What is the purpose of using macros in Vim?

    A. To automate repetitive tasks

    B. To change the syntax highlighting of a file

    C. To navigate between files in Vim

    D. To customize the Vim interface

    Answer: A

5) How can a user save a macro in Vim to use it in other sessions?

      A. By copying and pasting the macro code to a separate file

      B. By saving the macro to the .vimrc file

      C. By saving the macro to a separate file and sourcing it in Vim

      D. By typing the macro code every time it is needed

      Answer: C

# A.3 Quiz - Using Vim for Coding

1) What command can be used to automatically indent a block of code in Vim?
- A. "V"
- B. ">"
- C. "gcc"
- D. "zf}"
- Answer: B

2) How can Vim automatically add a comment to a line of code?
- A. "V"
- B. ">"
- C. "gcc"
- D. "zf}"
- Answer: C

3) Which command can be used to fold a section of code in Vim?
- A. "V"
- B. ">"
- C. "gcc"
- D. "zf}"
- Answer: D

4) How can Vim be customized to automatically indent code based on user preferences?
- A. By using plugins
- B. By using the ">>" command
- C. By using the "gcc" command
- D. By modifying the .vimrc file
- Answer: D

5) What is the purpose of code folding in Vim?
    A. To save disk space
    B. To improve code readability
    C. To increase program performance
    D. To remove unnecessary code
    Answer: B

# Appendix B - Vim Cheat Sheet

**Vim Modes:**

- **Normal Mode**: The default mode for navigating and manipulating text.
- **Insert Mode**: Used for inserting and editing text.
- **Visual Mode**: Used for selecting and manipulating text visually.
- **Command-Line Mode**: Used for entering Vim commands.

**Navigation in Normal Mode:**

- **h**: Move cursor left.
- **j**: Move cursor down.
- **k**: Move cursor up.
- **l**: Move cursor right.
- **w**: Move to the beginning of the next word.
- **b**: Move to the beginning of the previous word.
- **0**: Move to the beginning of the line.
- **$**: Move to the end of the line.
- **gg**: Go to the start of the document.
- **G**: Go to the end of the document.
- **{number}G**: Go to a specific line number.

**Inserting and Editing Text:**

- **i**: Insert before the cursor.
- **I**: Insert at the beginning of the line.
- **a**: Insert after the cursor.
- **A**: Insert at the end of the line.
- **o**: Open a new line below the current line.
- **O**: Open a new line above the current line.
- **x**: Delete the character under the cursor.
- **dd**: Delete the current line.
- **yy**: Copy the current line.
- **p**: Paste after the cursor.

**Saving and Quitting:**

- **:w**: Save changes.
- **:q**: Quit Vim.
- **:q!**: Quit Vim without saving.
- **:wq**: Save changes and quit.
- **:x**: Save changes and quit (similar to :wq).

**Undo and Redo:**

- **u**: Undo the last change.
- **Ctrl-r**: Redo the last undone action.

**Searching and Replacing:**

- **/pattern**: Search forward for `pattern`.
- **?pattern**: Search backward for `pattern`.
- **n**: Move to the next search result.
- **N**: Move to the previous search result.
- **:%s/pattern/replacement/g**: Replace all occurrences of `pattern` with `replacement`.

**Copy and Paste (Visual Mode):**

- **v**: Start Visual Mode for character-wise selection.
- **V**: Start Visual Mode for line-wise selection.
- **y**: Yank (copy) the selected text.
- **d**: Delete the selected text.
- **p**: Paste the yanked or deleted text.

**File Operations (Command-Line Mode):**

- **:e filename**: Edit a specific file.
- **:w filename**: Write (save) the file with a new name.
- **:wq**: Save changes and quit.
- **:q!**: Quit without saving changes.
- **:e!**: Revert to the last saved version of the file.

**Split Windows:**

- **:split**: Split the window horizontally.
- **:vsplit**: Split the window vertically.
- **Ctrl-w, w**: Switch between split windows.
- **Ctrl-w, q**: Close the current split window.

Remember that Vim has many more commands and features, and this cheat sheet covers only the basics. As you become more familiar with Vim, you can explore advanced features and customize your configuration to enhance your productivity further.

# Appendix C - Access to Online Course

You can use the following link to get free access to this class on my website:

https://www.destinlearning.com/courses/vim-essentials?coupon=VIM2024

If you have any difficulty registering, please contact me at:

sales@destinlearning.com